T0148597

DRAWING STARS
and
BUILDING POLYHEDRA

Written by **Christopher M. Freeman**
Illustrated by **Stephanie O'Shaughnessy**

Reproduction rights granted for single-classroom use only.

First published 2005 by Prufrock Press Inc.

Published 2021 by Routledge
605 Third Avenue, New York, NY 10017
2 Park Square, Milton Park, Abingdon, Oxon OX14 4RN

Routledge is an imprint of the Taylor & Francis Group, an informa business

© 2005 by Taylor & Francis

All rights reserved. No part of this book may be reprinted or reproduced or utilised in any form or by any electronic, mechanical, or other means, now known or hereafter invented, including photocopying and recording, or in any information storage or retrieval system, without permission in writing from the publishers.

Notice:
Product or corporate names may be trademarks or registered trademarks and are used only for identification and explanation without intent to infringe.

ISBN 13: 978-1-59363-066-9 (pbk)

Edited by Dianne Draze

Routledge
Taylor & Francis Group
NEW YORK AND LONDON

Contents

Drawing Stars

Introduction · · · · · · · · · · · · · · · · · 5
Lesson Notes · · · · · · · · · · · · · · · · 7
Name Game · · · · · · · · · · · · · · · · · 11
Record Sheet · · · · · · · · · · · · · · · · 12
1 - What is a Star? · · · · · · · · · · · · · 13
2 - Drawing Stars · · · · · · · · · · · · · 17
3 - Stars With 8 Points · · · · · · · · · · · 20
4 - Stars with 9 Points · · · · · · · · · · · 22
5 - Stars with 10 or 11 Points · · · · · · · 25
6 - Stars with 12 or 13 Points · · · · · · · 27
7 - Stars with 14 or 15 Points · · · · · · · 29
8 - Stars With 30 Points · · · · · · · · · · 31
9 - Extra Challenge · · · · · · · · · · · · · 33
10 - Stars on Flags · · · · · · · · · · · · · 35
Answer Key · · · · · · · · · · · · · · · · · 36

Building Polyhedra

Teacher's Notes · · · · · · · · · · · · · · · 39
1 - Dodecahedron · · · · · · · · · · · · · · 42
2 - Tetrahedron, Octahedron, Icosahedron · · 43
3 - Cube · · · · · · · · · · · · · · · · · · · 45
Data Recorder · · · · · · · · · · · · · · · · 46
Implications · · · · · · · · · · · · · · · · · 47
4 - Dual Combination Polyhedra · · · · · · · 48
5 - Truncated Polyhedra · · · · · · · · · · · 50
6 - Prisms, Antiprisms, and Pyramids · · · · · 52
7 - Stellated Polyhedra · · · · · · · · · · · 53
8 - Rhombic Polyhedra · · · · · · · · · · · 54
9 - Filling Space · · · · · · · · · · · · · · · 55
Polygon Masters · · · · · · · · · · · · · · · 56
Answer Key · · · · · · · · · · · · · · · · · 64

Dedication

This book is dedicated to my wife Maria, who is my best friend, to our three children, Clara, Edward, and John, who all love to draw stars, and to my mother, Maeda, whose tender, loving care remains with us always.

Acknowledgments

I am grateful to Joan Franklin Smutny, whose Worlds of Wisdom and Wonder programs for gifted students have provided many opportunities for me to share mathematical delight with children. I am also grateful to Garrett Derner, with whom I first investigated the mathematics of stars.

Drawing Stars
Introduction

What Will Students Do?

As students work independently through a series of lessons, they will learn to draw stars with any number of points — 7-pointed, 8-pointed, 9-pointed, and stars with larger numbers of points. For example:

What Math Will They Learn?

As a result of doing these exercises students will develop a definition of star, and they will practice inductive thinking by formulating conjectures about the structure of stars. In particular, students will learn to predict whether a star will be continuous or will be composed of overlapping figures (like the one in the center above, which is three overlapping pentagrams). Every overlapping star illustrates a multiplication fact (in this case, 3 x 5 = 15). Students will discover that the greatest common factor is the key to understanding the structure of stars.

Which NTCM Standards Does This Activity Address?

Number and Operations
- Grades 3-5 - understand various meanings of multiplication and division
- Grades 6-8 - use factors and relatively prime numbers to solve problems

Geometry
- Grades 3-5 - make and test conjectures about geometric relationships
- Grades 6-8 - create and critique inductive and deductive arguments concerning geometric ideas and relationships
- Grades K-12 - analyze characteristics and properties of two- and three-dimensional geometric shapes and develop mathematical arguments about geometric relationships

Reasoning and Proof
- Grades K-12 - make and investigate mathematical conjectures

Connections
- Grades K-12 - recognize and apply mathematics in contexts outside of mathematics

How Much Time Will It Take?

Students will work from 8 to 12 hours to complete all the lessons.

What Materials Will I Need?

You will need to have the following materials:
- copies of each lesson in this book, one for each student
- at least one copy of the 30-pointed star (page 32) for each student
- rulers (6″ is ideal), one for each student
- pencils
- colored pencils
- markers
- record sheet (page 12)

Classroom Management

On the first day with new students, play a name game with a beanbag. This is described in the introductory lesson on page 11. Many key concepts about drawing stars are exemplified by specific rules for how to toss the bag.

After the first day, students can work independently and at their own pace on the various lessons. When a student finishes a lesson, he or she turns it in and starts work on the next lesson. Check each student's work as it is turned in. Consult about any necessary corrections and keep a record of each student's progress.

Lesson notes for each lesson are provided. These notes give you questions to guide students through the inductive process. They may also be used as lesson guides if you prefer to structure your class in a more teacher-guided, less independent work fashion.

After Lesson 8, assign a different 30-pointed star to each student. Check their line drawings and encourage them to color them in ways that illustrate their structure. The finished stars can be displayed on the wall in order by "over" number.

Field Testing

For many years, I have taught students in grades 3-6 how to draw stars. I developed these lessons for my classes in the Worlds of Wisdom and Wonder programs sponsored by the Center for Gifted at National-Louis University in the Chicago area. I have also used these lessons as an elective activity with my sixth graders at the University of Chicago Laboratory Schools. Each time the lessons have been revised to facilitate students' independent learning and higher-order thinking.

Drawing Stars

Lesson Notes

Introductory Lesson   Follow the detailed instructions for the Name Game on page 11.

Lesson 1

What Is a Star?

Objective:
Students will attempt to draw stars and will devise a systematic procedure.

Procedure:
Start by drawing a 5-pointed star on the board and ask, "What are the points of this star?"

Then draw a figure like the one on the right.
Ask, "Is this a point?" (No, it's an angle.)

Point out that the points of a star are the places where the line segments touch. Points are very tiny, but we often represent them with dots.

Hand out lesson 1, pages 13-16.

This lesson is intended to be a whole-class activity. Give the students enough time to try drawing their own stars, and then discuss the questions with the whole group.

Discuss why each example is or is not a good example of a star. For each one, ask "What is wrong with this star?"

Ask student what procedures they think they should use to draw "good" stars. Guide them toward the procedures presented in lesson 2.

When students draw stars, in this lesson and all subsequent lessons, stress that they need to use rulers.

Lesson 2

How Do You Draw Stars?

Objective:
Students will draw all the 6-pointed and 7-pointed stars and observe that different "over" numbers may produce the same star.

Procedure:
Hand out lesson 2, pages 17-19.

From this lesson on, students may work at their own pace. When a student completes a lesson, collect the work and give him or her the packet of materials for the next lesson. Grade each lesson, record the score, and discuss any corrections with the student.

You may wish to point out that the 4-pointed star "over 2" and the 6-pointed star "over 3" are "asterisks." "Aster" means "star" in Greek, and "asterisk" means "little star" or "starlet." In any asterisk, each point is connected to just one other point. For other stars, each point is connected to two other points.

You may need to reassure students that it is <u>not possible</u> to draw a 6-pointed star "over 6."

Lesson 3

How Many Stars Are There?

Objective:
Students will draw all of the 8-pointed stars and make a conjecture that predicts which "over numbers" produce the same star.

Procedure:
When a student finishes lesson 2, give him or her lesson 3 (pages 20-21) and have the student work independently on the exercises.

If a student is stumped by question 7, ask him or her to play this game: Say, "I will tell you a particular *even* number of points. How would you compute how many stars there are with that number of points?" (answer: divide by 2)

When a student correctly answers that question, play this game: Say, "Suppose I tell you a particular *odd* number of points. How would you compute how many stars there are with that *odd* number of points?" (answer: divide by 2 and subtract ½ or divide by 2 and round down)

As an extension ask, "Which numbers of points have asterisks?" (answer: only even numbers of points)

Lesson 4

How Do Stars Illustrate Multiplication?

Objective:
Students will draw all the 9-pointed stars, distinguish continuous stars from overlapping stars, and describe the structure of a star with a multiplication fact.

Procedure:
When a student finishes lesson 3, hand out copies of pages 22-24 and let him or her work independently on the exercises.

Vocabulary reminder (factor and product):
factor x factor = product
During this lesson students should also discover that when using multiplication sentences to describe a star, the order of the factors is important, although they have the same product.

After completing the worksheets, you may wish to ask students what other interesting aspects of these stars they notice. This is a very open-ended question; there are lots of correct answers.

Lesson 5

Are You Sure You Know Which Stars Are Continuous?

Objective:
Students will draw all of the 10-pointed and 11-pointed stars and use them to make and test conjectures about which "over numbers" produce overlapping stars and which produce continuous stars.

Procedure:
When a student finishes lesson 4, hand out copies of pages 25-26 and let him or her work independently.

Vocabulary reminder:
factor
A number can be divided by its factor without leaving a remainder.

Students often presume that for a star to be overlapping the "over number" must be a factor of the number of points. Most students are very surprised when the 10-pointed star "over 4" is overlapping. Point out to students that they will be asked to refine their conjecture in the next few lessons.

Many students presume that all the 11-pointed stars are continuous because 11 is odd. Point out that 9 is also odd, but the 9-pointed star "over 3" is overlapping. Oddness is not the key.

Lesson 6

How Do Factors Determine the Structure of a Star?

Objective:
Students will draw all of the 12-pointed stars and the 13-pointed stars and establish two correct generalizations about the structure of stars.

Procedure:
After a student completes lesson 5, hand out pages 27-28 and let him or her work independently on lesson 6.

You may need to remind students that the order of the factors is important.
$3 \times 4 = 12$ means three overlapping 4-pointed stars.
$4 \times 3 = 12$ means four overlapping 3-pointed stars.

Lesson 7

How Does the GCF Predict the Structure of a Star?

Objective:
Students will draw all of the 14-pointed stars and make a generalization that uses the greatest common factor of the "over number" and the number of points to predict the structure of the star.

Procedure:
After a student completes lesson 6, hand out pages 29-30 and let him or her work independently on lesson 7.

Review the greatest common factor and relatively prime numbers. Give additional examples of both if necessary.

Lesson 8

Making Generalizations about Stars

Objective:
Students will complete a chart that uses the greatest common factor (GCF) to predict the structure of all the different 30-pointed stars. Each student will also draw a different 30-pointed star to display on the wall.

Procedure:
When a student finishes lesson 7, hand out the chart on page 31.

When several students have completed the chart, give everyone the 30-pointed star on page 32. Let them take a break from the other lessons while they prepare their stars for display.

Have each student draw a different 30-pointed star. Assign each student a different "over number" between 1 and 15 (or larger if you have more students). The closer the "over number" is to 15, the more complicated the star will be, so ask students how much challenge they want. Keep a record of which number is assigned to which student and don't let two students draw the same "over numbers."

It is a good idea to check students' pencil-drawn stars before they color them. Have the students select a color scheme that emphasizes the structure of their star and insist that they work carefully.

Display the 30-pointed stars on the wall in order of increasing "over numbers." This will take 12 feet of wall space or more. Students who work more slowly through the lessons will appreciate having the 30-pointed stars on display to check their work on the chart later.

Students may notice that within each star may be found all the stars with smaller "over numbers."

Lesson 9

Extra Challenge

This is a lesson for students who are capable and who want an extra challenge.

Objective:
Students will make additional generalizations about the structure of stars.

Procedure:
When students finish lesson 8, determine if they are willing to try an additional challenge. If so, hand out pages 33-34.

Additional question to ask:
Every prime number has exactly two factors, itself and 1. You have seen that prime numbers of points have all their stars continuous. Numbers that have three or more factors may have stars that are "composed" of overlapping figures. What word do we use in math for the numbers that have three or more factors? (Answer: composite)

A Real Challenge:
If you know the number of points, p, and the "over number," n, of a star, can you figure out a way to compute the measure of the angle of each point?

Hint:
Use the 10-pointed star "over 3" as a special case. Every star can be inscribed into a circle. The measure of the full circle is 360º. A piece of a circle is called an arc. The measure of the little arc between two successive points is 360/10 or 36º. Four of these little arcs put together measures 36 x 4 = 144º. Every angle of the star is also inscribed into a circle (an "inscribed angle" has its vertex on the circle). Every inscribed angle intercepts an arc of the circle (dark in the picture). For this star, we just computed the measure of the intercepted arc to be 144º. There is a theorem from geometry that the measure of an inscribed angle is half the measure of its intercepted arc. Therefore, for this 10-pointed star "over 3," the measure of each angle of each point is half of 144, or 72º.

Lesson 10

Objective:
Students will identify the structure of stars on national flags.

Procedure:
Many countries use stars on their national flags. Ask students to look up the flags of the following countries in an encyclopedia, an atlas or on the Internet. Once they find the flags, have them identify what type of star is on the flag, writing their answers on page 35.

Name Game

Objective

This game helps students learn everyone's name and develop a strong intuition for how to draw stars.

Getting Started

You need an object to toss around — a soft ball or beanbag. Seat the students in a ring so everyone can see everyone else. If there happens to be a prime number of students, the teacher should join the ring as well.

Round 1

When the ball is tossed to someone, the receiver must say his or her name. The tosser then says, "I just tossed the ball to _____". Demonstrate by tossing the ball to a student, and then let the students toss to each other.

Round 2

A player may toss the ball only to someone whose name he or she knows. Before tossing, say, "I'm tossing the ball to _____." Demonstrate and then let the students toss to each other. When everyone has received the ball once, begin the next round.

Round 3

Tell students to count to their left seven people. When they receive the ball say, "I'm tossing the ball to _____" and toss the ball to that person. If the number of people in the ring happens to be a multiple of 7, then count over 6 instead. Toss the ball to a student to start. When the ball gets back to the starting student, go on to round four.

Round 4

Select another number that is a factor of the number of people in the ring. Modify the rules of round 3 so as to count over this new number. Begin throwing the ball. When the ball gets back to the starting student, ask whether everyone has received the ball once. When students say "no," ask how many have received the ball. Students may observe that the "over number" times the number that have received the ball equals the number of people in the ring. Ask how to ensure that every person gets the ball once. They will suggest handing the ball to the next player in line to start another circuit. Let them continue until everyone has received the ball once.

Further Rounds

If time permits, play further rounds with different "over numbers." You may also want to reverse direction.

Follow Up

Draw two circles of points on the board, each with the same number of points as there are people in the ring. Each point represents a person and each connection represents a toss. Show how to draw a star by counting "over" the same number of points each time, naming students as you proceed. Round three will illustrate a continuous star, while round four will illustrate an overlapping star.

Drawing Stars

Record Sheet

Record students names in the first column and their scores for each lesson in the columns to the right of their names. Grade each lesson + +, +, ✓, or – .

students' names	1	2	3	4	5	6	7	8	9	10	comments

© Prufrock Press Inc. - *Drawing Stars, Building Polyhedra*

What is a Star?

Name _____

Examples of Stars

These stars you probably already know how to draw.

5 points
pentagram

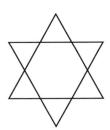

6 points
Star of David

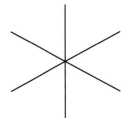

6 points
asterisk

This one may be new to you:

7 points

Try It Out

Try drawing several stars with seven or eight points.

Defining Stars

Stars are points that are connected with line segments ("segments" for short). The points of a star are the endpoints of the segments used to draw it.

• point

 line segment

One possible way to draw a star would be to locate its points first.

Then connect them with segments, like this.

1. Is this a good-looking star? Why?

_____

_____

2. Should all the points of a star be the same distance from the center? _____

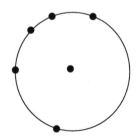

What if you locate your points on a circle and then connect them with segments like this?

3. Does this look like a star? Why? _____

_____

© Prufrock Press Inc. - *Drawing Stars, Building Polyhedra*

4. Suppose we locate our points equally spaced around the circle, like this:

But then we connect the points like this:

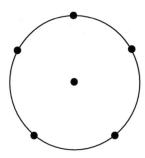

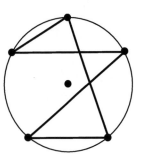

What's wrong with this star?_____

_____

5. Here are some pictures of 7 and 8 points, equally spaced around a circle. Try to draw good-looking stars using these points.

Seven points

Eight points

6. What systematic procedure can we follow to connect the points so that the star looks as good as possible?

_____

_____

7. Here are some more circles of points for you to test your ideas about drawing stars.

Seven points

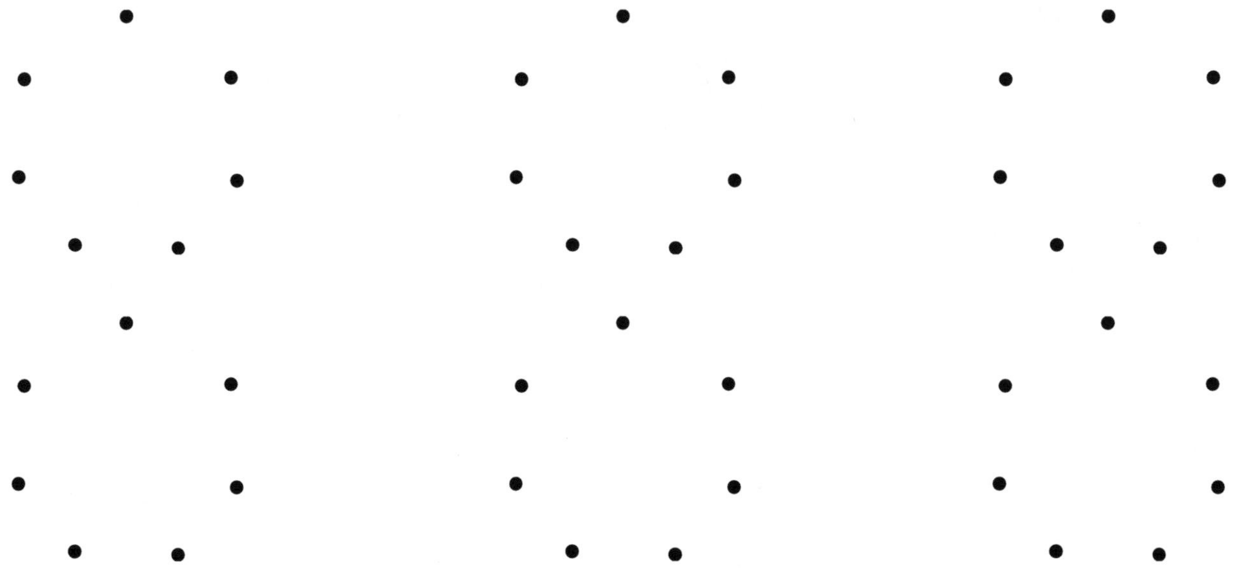

Eight points

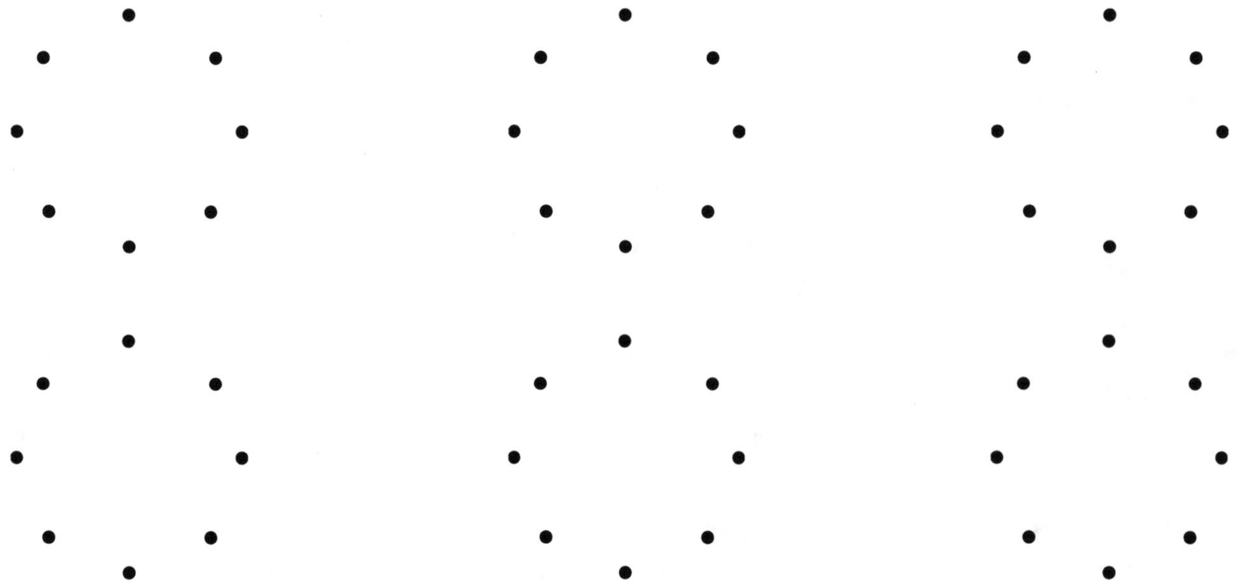

© Prufrock Press Inc. - *Drawing Stars, Building Polyhedra*

Drawing Stars

Name _____

Procedure

- Start with any number of points equally spaced around a circle.
- Choose a starting point. Count over a certain number of points to find another point. Connect the two points with a segment.
- From a new starting point, count over the same number of points to find another point. Connect the two points with a segment.
- Continue connecting points, always counting over the same number each time, until every point is connected to two other points or maybe to just one other point.

Examples

Using this procedure, you will find that:

There is only one 2-pointed star.

And there is only one 3-pointed star.

But there are two different-looking 4-pointed stars.

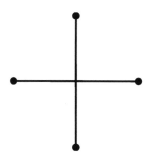

"over 1"
This star is called over 1, because each point is connected to the first point next to it around the circle.

"over 2"
This star is over 2, because each point is connected to the second point around the circle.

There are two 5-pointed stars.

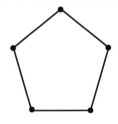

"over 1"
pentagon

"over 2"
pentagram

Try It Out

1. Finish the 6-pointed stars below. For the first star, connect each point to the one next to it. For the second star, count "over 2" points and connect them. For the third star, count "over 3" points. Begin with the point 0.

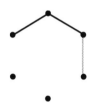

"over 1"
hexagon

"over 2"
2 overlapping triangles

"over 3"
3 overlapping segments

2. See what happens when you try to draw 6-pointed stars by counting "over 4," "over 5," and "over 6."

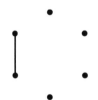

"over 4"

"over 5"

"over 6"

© Prufrock Press Inc. - *Drawing Stars, Building Polyhedra*

Investigate

3. Which pairs of "over numbers" produce 6-pointed stars that look the same?

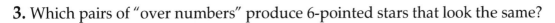

4. How many different-looking 6-pointed stars are there? _____

5. Draw all the 7-pointed stars.

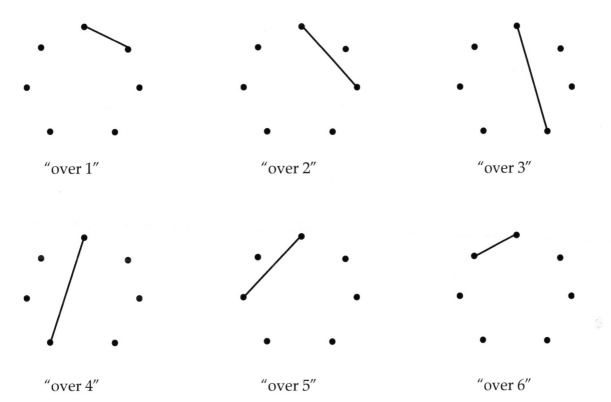

"over 1"   "over 2"   "over 3"

"over 4"   "over 5"   "over 6"

6. How many different-looking 7-pointed stars are there? _____

7. Which pairs of "over numbers" produce 7-pointed stars that look the same?

_____

8. How do the "over numbers" in each pair relate to each other?

_____

Stars with 8 Points

Name _____

Investigate

Draw these 8-pointed stars. You will find that the "over 2" star consists of two overlapping squares. Use a colored pencil to draw the second square in a different color.

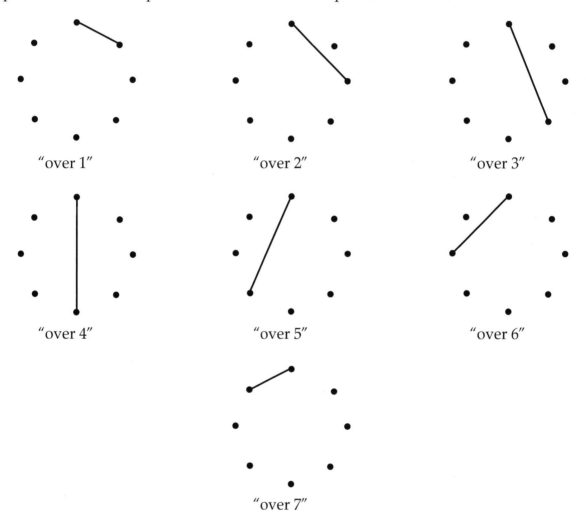

"over 1"   "over 2"   "over 3"

"over 4"   "over 5"   "over 6"

"over 7"

Observations

1. How many different-looking 8-pointed stars are there? _____

2. List all pairs of "over numbers" that produce the same 8-pointed stars.

_____

3. What is the sum of each pair of "over numbers"? _____

 © Prufrock Press Inc. - *Drawing Stars, Building Polyhedra*

Conjectures

Now you are ready to make some conjectures about stars. These conjectures will be statements you think are true about all stars, based on your observations of the few you have drawn.

4. For 6-pointed stars, if two "over numbers" add up to 6, they produce the same star.
For 7-pointed stars, if two "over numbers" add up to 7, they produce the same star.
For 8-pointed stars, if two "over numbers" add up to 8, they produce the same star.
For stars with any number of points, what can you say about their "over numbers"?

_____

_____

5. According to your conjecture, if you draw all the 9-pointed stars, which "over numbers" would produce the same star?

"over 1" would produce the same star as _____

"over 2" would produce the same star as _____

"over 3" would produce the same star as _____

"over 4" would produce the same star as _____

How many different-looking 9-pointed stars do you expect there to be? _____

6. Think about all the stars you have drawn. For each number of points, how many different-looking stars are there?

    _1_ 2-pointed star   _1_ 3-pointed star

    _2_ 4-pointed stars   _____ 5-pointed stars

    _____ 6-pointed stars   _____ 7-pointed stars

    _____ 8-pointed stars   _____ 9-pointed stars

7. If you know the number of points, how can you tell how many stars there are with that number of points? _____

_____

Stars with 9 Points

Name _____

Definition

Several stars are composed of overlapping copies of stars with fewer points. These are **overlapping** stars. Every overlapping star illustrates a multiplication fact.

Examples

This 4-pointed star "over 2" is composed of two overlapping 2-pointed stars. This star illustrates the multiplication fact 2 x 2 = 4.

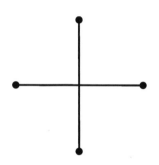

4 points "over 2"
2 x 2 = 4

The 6-pointed star "over 2" is composed of two overlapping 3-pointed stars. This star illustrates the multiplication fact 2 x 3 = 6. But the 6-pointed star "over 3" is composed of three overlapping 2-pointed stars. This star illustrates 3 x 2 = 6.

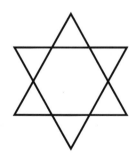

6 points "over 2"
2 x 3 = 6

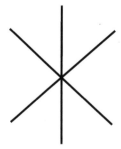

6 points "over 3"
3 x 2 = 6

When writing a multiplication fact for a star, the first factor tells how many overlapping stars it is composed of, and the second factor tells how many points each of these overlapping stars has.

 © Prufrock Press Inc. - *Drawing Stars, Building Polyhedra*

Try It Out

1. What does 3 x 4 = 12 mean in this context? *(choose the best definition)*
   a. Three overlapping four-pointed stars.
   b. Four overlapping three-pointed stars.
   c. Twelve overlapping four-pointed stars, each "over 3."

2. Here is an 8-pointed star "over 2." It is composed of two overlapping 4-pointed stars. What multiplication fact does it illustrate?

3. Draw the star that illustrates the multiplication fact 4 x 2 = 8.

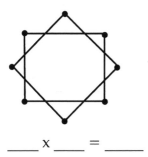

____ x ____ = ____

Definition

Many stars are **not** composed of overlapping copies. Such stars can be drawn with straight segments from point to point without lifting the pencil. They are **continuous stars**. Every continuous star illustrates the multiplication fact **1 x p = p**, where p is the number of points.

Examples

3 points "over 1"
1 x 3 = 3

5 points "over 1"
1 x 5 = 5

5 points "over 2"
1 x 5 = 5

Observations

4. Which "over numbers" in the 6-pointed stars produce continuous stars? _____

5. Which "over numbers" in the 7-pointed stars produce continuous stars? _____

6. Are there any 7-pointed stars that are overlapping? _____

Investigate

7. Draw all of the 9-pointed stars. Below each star write the multiplication fact that describes its structure.

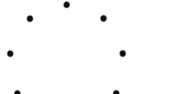

"over 1"

_____

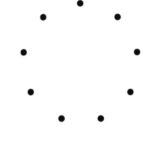

"over 2"

_____

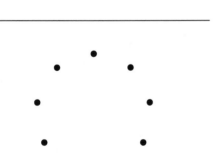

"over 3"

_____

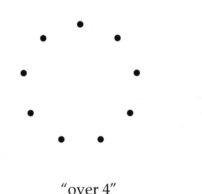

"over 4"

_____

8. Which "over numbers" produce overlapping 9-pointed stars? _____

9. What special relationship do the numbers 3 and 9 have? _____

_____

   © Prufrock Press Inc. - *Drawing Stars, Building Polyhedra*

Lesson 5 Stars with 10 or 11 Points

Name _____

Make a Conjecture

1. Before you draw the 10-pointed stars, predict which "over numbers" you think will produce overlapping stars. _____

Test Your Ideas

2. Draw the 10-pointed stars and check your predictions. On the blank line below each "over number," write the multiplication fact that describes the composition of that star.

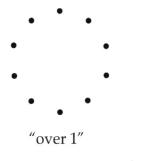

"over 1"

_____

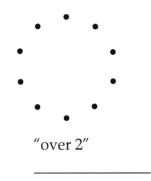

"over 2"

_____

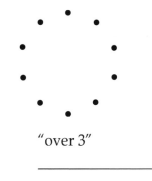

"over 3"

_____

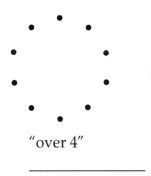

"over 4"

_____

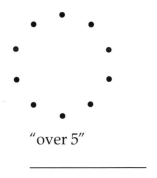

"over 5"

_____

3. Were your predictions correct? If not, which star was different than you thought?

_____

4. What do the numbers 4 and 10 have in common that makes the 10-pointed star "over 4" overlapping rather than continuous? _____

Make a Conjecture

5. Before you draw the 11-pointed stars, predict which "over numbers" you think will produce overlapping stars. _____

Test Your Ideas

6. Draw the 11-pointed stars and check your predictions. On the blank line below each "over number," write the multiplication fact that describes the composition of that star.

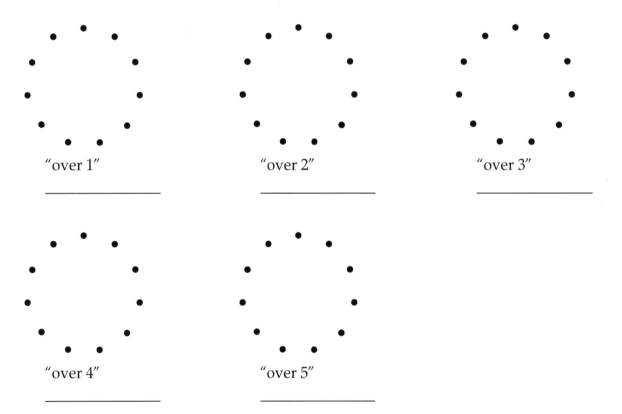

"over 1"

_____

"over 2"

_____

"over 3"

_____

"over 4"

_____

"over 5"

_____

7. Were your predictions correct? If not, which star was different than you thought?

_____

8. Look at all the stars you have drawn. If all stars with the number of points listed below are continuous, circle the number.

    2   3   4   5   6   7   8   9   10   11

9. What special quality does the number 11 have that makes all its stars continuous?

_____

© Prufrock Press Inc. - *Drawing Stars, Building Polyhedra*

Stars with 12 or 13 Points

Name _____

Make a Conjecture

1. What are all the factors of 12? _____

2. Before you draw the 12-pointed stars, predict which "over numbers" you think will produce overlapping stars. _____

Test Your Ideas

3. Use colored pencils to draw the 12-pointed stars and check your predictions.
If the star is overlapping, make each overlapping figure a different color.
Write the multiplication fact that describes the composition of that star.

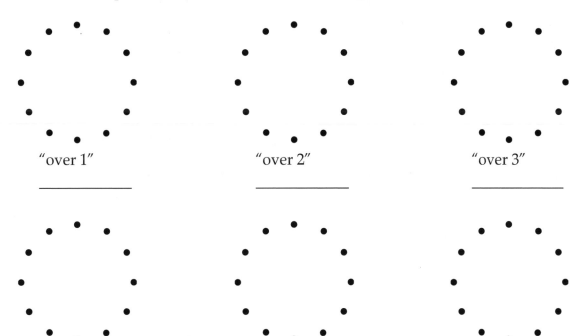

"over 1"
_____

"over 2"
_____

"over 3"
_____

"over 4"
_____

"over 5"
_____

"over 6"
_____

Make a Generalization

4. Complete the statement below so it is true.

If the "over number" (except _____) is a factor of the number of points, then the star is overlapping.

Definition

A **prime number** is a number that has only two factors, itself and one.
The number 13 is prime.

Make a Conjecture

5. Before you draw these 13-pointed stars, predict which "over numbers" will produce
continuous stars. _____

Test Your Ideas

6. Draw the 13-pointed stars and check your predictions.

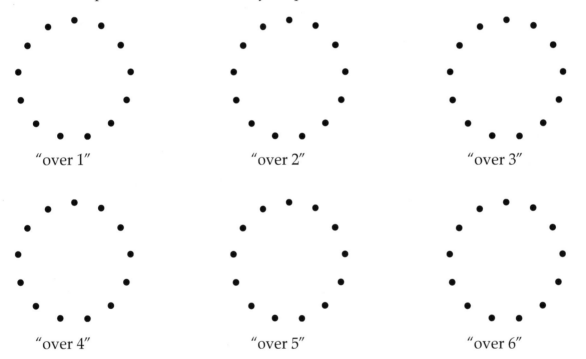

"over 1"   "over 2"   "over 3"

"over 4"   "over 5"   "over 6"

Make a Generalization

7. Were your predictions correct? If not, which stars were different than you expected?

_____

8. What do you suppose is true about all stars with a prime number of points?
Finish this sentence.

All stars with a prime number of points are _____.

Stars with 14 or 15 Points

Name _____

Drawing 14-Pointed Stars

★ Draw these 14-pointed stars.

★ Use colored pencils to emphasize overlapping figures.

★ On the blank below each star, write the multiplication fact that describes it.

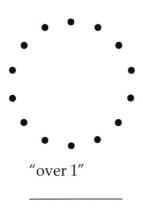

"over 1"

_____

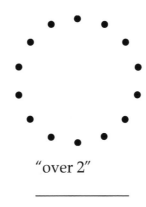

"over 2"

_____

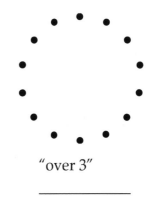

"over 3"

_____

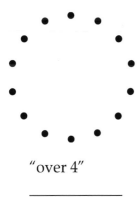

"over 4"

_____

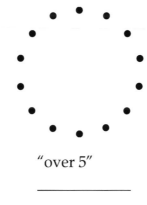

"over 5"

_____

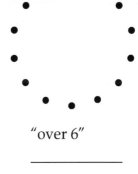

"over 6"

_____

"over 7"

_____

Definition

The **greatest common factor** (GCF) of two numbers is the largest number that is a factor of both of the numbers.

Two numbers are **relatively prime** if their greatest common factor is 1.

Applying the Definition

1. The greatest common factor (GCF) of 14 and 4 is 2.
How many overlapping figures compose a 14-pointed star "over 4"? _____

2. What is the GCF of 14 and 6? _____
How many overlapping figures compose a 14-pointed star "over 6"? _____

3. What is the GCF of 14 and 7? _____
How many overlapping figures compose a 14-pointed star "over 7"? _____

4. What is the GCF of 14 and 3? _____
What kind of star is a 14-pointed star "over 3"? _____

Make a Generalization

5. Complete this sentence.
If the greatest common factor of the number of points and the "over number" is 1,
then the star is _____

6. Complete this sentence.
If the greatest common factor of the number of points and the "over number" is greater
than 1, then the star is _____

and the GCF tells you _____

Test Your Generalization

7. Does your generalization correctly
predict the structure of this 15-pointed
star over 6? _____

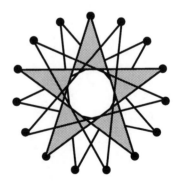

      © Prufrock Press Inc. - *Drawing Stars, Building Polyhedra*

Stars with 30 Points

Name _____

Generalizations

If the greatest common factor of the number of points and the "over number" is 1, then the star is continuous.

If the greatest common factor of the number of points and the "over number" is greater than 1, then the greatest common factor tells the number of overlapping figures.

Use these generalizations to predict the composition of 30-pointed stars. Fill in this table.

over number	GCF of over number and 30	structure you predict	multiplication fact
over 1	1	continuous	1 x 30 = 30
over 2	2	two 15-pointed stars	2 x 15
over 3	3		
over 4		two 15-pointed stars	
over 5			5 x 6
over 6			
over 7		continuous	
over 8			
over 9			
over 10			
over 11			
over 12			
over 13			
over 14			
over 15			

Stars with 30 Points

Name _____

★ This picture has 30 points equally spaced around a circle.

★ Select an "over number" and draw a large 30-pointed star. Use a ruler.

★ Color your star with colored pencils or markers. Select a color pattern that emphasizes the structure of the star.

★ Below the star, write the "over number" and the multiplication fact the star illustrates.

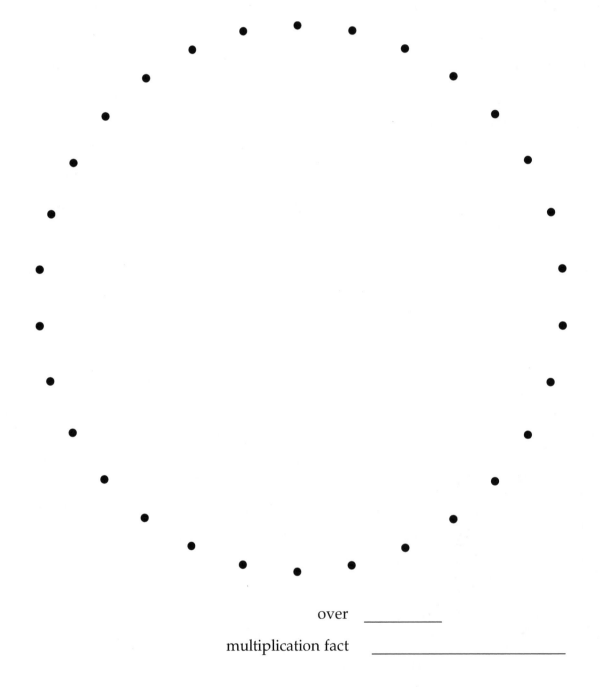

over _____

multiplication fact _____

  © *Prufrock Press Inc. - Drawing Stars, Building Polyhedra*

Extra Challenge
For Experts

Name _____

Investigate

Study these stars to see how the greatest common factor (GCF) of the "over number" and the number of points can tell you the **type** of overlapping figures.

14 points "over 4"
GCF = 2
two 7-pointed stars
each "over 2"

14 points "over 6"
GCF = 2
two 7-pointed stars
each "over 3"

30 points "over 12"
GCF = 6
six 5-point stars
each "over 2"

Make a Generalization

1. State two rules to describe the structure of the overlapping figures.

You can use the GCF of the number of points and the "over number" of a star to determine the number of points each overlapping figure has by _____

_____

You can use the GCF of the number of points and the "over number" of a star to determine the "over number" of each overlapping figure by _____

_____

Testing Generalizations

Consider this 15-pointed star "over 6".

2. Use your first rule to explain
why this figure is composed of five-pointed stars.

_____

3. Use your second rule to explain why those five-pointed stars are each "over 2".

_____

Consider this 30-pointed star "over 9".

4. Use the GCF to explain how many overlapping
figures this star is composed of. _____

_____

_____

5. Use your first rule to explain how many points
each overlapping figure has. _____

_____

_____

6. Use your second rule to explain the "over number" of each overlapping figure.

_____

 © Prufrock Press Inc. - *Drawing Stars, Building Polyhedra*

Stars on Flags

Many countries use stars on their national flags. In this lesson, you will identify the types of stars used by 16 countries. Look up these flags in an atlas, in an encyclopedia, or on the Internet. For each flag, tell the number of points on the "over number."

United States of America

__5__ points, over __2__

Burkina Faso

_____ points, over _____

Israel

_____ points, over _____

Jordan

_____ points, over _____

Azerbaijan

_____ points, over _____

Namibia

_____ points, over _____

Nepal

_____ points, over _____

Antigua and Barbuda

_____ points, over _____

Morocco

_____ points, over _____

Cameroon

_____ points, over _____

Burundi

_____ points, over _____

Australia

_____ points, over _____

and

_____ points, over _____

and

_____ points, over _____

(This flag has three types of stars.)

Taiwan

_____ points, over _____

Naura

_____ points, over _____

Malaysia

_____ points, over _____

(hint: None of these stars are asterisks.)

Marshall Islands

_____ points, over _____

Drawing Stars Answers

Lesson 1

1. No, because one point is too far away from the others.
2. Yes An artist might like some points far out and others close in, but to make the mathematics easier, we will require all points to be the same distance from the center.
3. No The star will look better if you space the points evenly around the circle.
4. This star is lopsided because the points were not connected in a systematic way.
6. To get the best-looking (most symmetric) star, when you are deciding which points to connect, always count "over" the same number each time.

Lesson 2

Lesson 2 and all following lessons are intended to be worked on individually. Let the students complete them at their own rates. Grade them, record scores, and return them to the students as promptly as you can.

1.

   "over 1"   "over 2"   "over 3"

2.   [dots]

   "over 4"   "over 5"   "over 6"

3. "over 1" and "over 5"; "over 2" and "over 4"
4. three
5.   [star]

   "over 1"   "over 2"   "over 3"

   "over 4"   "over 5"   "over 6"

6. three
7. "over 1" and "over 6"; "over 2" and "over 5"; "over 3" and "over 4"
8. Each pair adds up to 7

Lesson 3

over 1 & 7   over 2 & 6   over 3 & 5   over 4

1. four
2. "over 1" and "over 7"; "over 2" and "over 6"; "over 3" and "over 5"
3. eight
4. If two "over numbers" add up to the number of points, they produce the same star.
5. "over 8"
   "over 7"
   "over 6"
   "over 5"
6. 1   1
   2   2
   3   3
   4   4
7. If the star has an even number of points, divide that number by two. If the star has an odd number of points, divide that number by two and subtract one half.

Lesson 4

1. a.
2. $2 \times 4 = 8$

3.

4. "over 1" and "over 5"
5. All of them
6. No
7.   [star]

   "over 1"   "over 2"   "over 3"   "over 4"
   $1 \times 9 = 9$ $1 \times 9 = 9$ $3 \times 3 = 9$ $1 \times 9 = 9$

8. just "over 3"
9. 3 is a factor of 9

Lesson 5

1. Answers will vary.

2.

"over 1"   "over 2"   "over 3"
1 x 10 = 10   2 x 5 = 10   1 x 10 = 10

"over 4"   "over 5"
2 x 5 = 10   5 x 2 = 10

3. Answers will vary; many students predict that "over 4" will be continuous, because four is not a factor of 10.

4. Both 4 and 10 are even numbers.

5. Answers will vary.

6.

"over 1"   "over 2"   "over 3"

"over 4"   "over 5"

7. Answers will vary.

8. 2, 3, 5, 7, and 11 should be circled.

9. 11 is prime, so its only multiplication fact is 1 x 11 = 11.

Lesson 6

1. 1, 2, 3, 4, 6, 12

2. Answers will vary.

3.

"over 1"   "over 2"   "over 3"
1 x 12 = 12   2 x 6 = 12   3 x 4 = 12

"over 4"   "over 5"   "over 6"
4 x 3 = 12   1 x 12 = 12   6 x 2 = 12

4. 1 is an exception; (so is 12, for 12-pointed stars).

5. Answers will vary.

6.

"over 1"'   "over 2"   "over 3"

"over 4"   "over 5"   "over 6"

7. Answers will vary.

8. All stars with a prime number of points are continuous.

Lesson 7

"over 1"   "over 2"   "over 3"
1 x 14   2 x 7   1 x 14

"over 4"   "over 5"   "over 6"
2 x 7   1 x 14   2 x 7

"over 7"
7 x 2

1. 2

2. 2, 2

3. 7, 7

4. 1, continuous

5. continuous

6. overlapping; the number of overlapping figures

7. yes

Lesson 8

over number	GCF	Prediction	Multiplication
1	1	continuous	1 x 30
2	2	2 15-point stars	2 x 15
3	3	3 10-point stars	3 x 10
4	2	2 15-point stars	2 x 15
5	5	5 6-point stars	5 x 6
6	6	6 5-point stars	6 x 5
7	1	continuous	1 x 30
8	2	2 15-point stars	2 x 15
9	3	3 10-point stars	3 x 10
10	10	10 3-point stars	10 x 3
11	1	continuous	1 x 30
12	6	6 5-point stars	6 x 5
13	1	continuous	1 x 30
14	2	2 15-point stars	2 x 15
15	15	15 2-point stars	15 x 2

Lesson 9

1. dividing the number of points in the star by the GCF.
   dividing the "over number" of the star by the GCF.
2. The GCF of 15 and 6 is 3; 15/3 = 5, so each overlapping figure has 5 points.
3. 6/3 = 2, so each overlapping figure is "over 2"
4. The GCF of 30 and 9 is 3, so there are three overlapping figures.
5. 30/3 = 10, so each overlapping figure has 10 points
6. 9/3 = 3, so each overlapping figure is "over 3"

Lesson 10

United States of America
5 points "over 2"

Burkina Faso
5 points "over 2"

Israel
6 points "over 2"

Jordan
7 points "over 2"

Azerbaijan
8 points "over 3"

Namibia
12 points "over 4"

Nepal
12 points "over 4"

Antigua and Barbuda
16 points "over 6"

Australia
8 points "over 2"
and 7 points "over 3"
and 5 points "over 2"

Morocco
5 points "over 2"

Cameroon
5 points "over 2"

Burundi
6 points "over 2"

Taiwan
12 points "over 5"

Nauru
12 points "over 5"

Malaysia
14 points "over 6"

Marshall Islands
24 points "over 11"

Building Polyhedra

Teaching Notes

What Will Students Do?

Students will spend each class cutting, folding, and stapling paper polygons into three-dimensional solids called polyhedra.

Why Build Polyhedra?

Building polyhedra is a kinesthetic activity involving spatial geometry. This is a motivating activity for students, ages 9–16. The activity addresses many educational needs:

- It involves students in a kinesthetic activity. Students learn by building.
- It invites inductive thinking. It involves learners in discovering the fundamental governing principles of how polygons fit together.
- It develops spatial intuition.
- It provides background essential to applications in crystal structure in chemistry and structural design in engineering.
- It fulfills the NCTM geometry standard, giving students an opportunity to "analyze characteristics and properties of two- and three-dimensional geometric shapes and develop mathematical arguments about geometric relationships."
- It's just plain fun.

What Are Polyhedra?

Polyhedra literally means "many faces" from the Greek. They are three-dimensional figures with flat surfaces, all of which are polygons. They are also called solids. In this activity, students will use only regular polygons—equilateral triangles, squares and regular pentagons, hexagons, octagons, and decagons.

How Much Time Does It Take?

You will find a lot of flexibility in the structure of these exercises. In two or three days students can build the five regular solids and investigate their properties. Given more time and a little direction, there are dozens of possible combinations students can discover for themselves.

Most students can build a dodecahedron in one 45-minute class period. Another class may be devoted to the other regular solids (tetrahedron, octahedron, icosahedron, and cube). You can have different students building different polyhedra. They will enjoy comparing what they built. The other polyhedra are suitable for an elective activity.

This class has been structured in different ways in different teaching situations. In one setting it was offered as a 45-minute activity period once a week for five weeks. In another program offered by the Center for Gifted it was taught for ten 50-minute classes. At another program for students in grades 6–10, the class was fifteen 70-minute classes. Students in this program had time for inverse stellation, space-filling, and using other materials beside paper, such as sticks and wire.

Materials

You will need the following materials for this unit. Collect all materials before beginning the unit.

- scissors - one pair for every two students
- mini-staplers - one for every two students. The shape of the base is critical. The front edge should be flat, not curved, and the lip between the front edge and the staple-bending groove should be as short as possible—¼ inch or less. Be sure to note which size staples your staplers use.
- extra staples - about 100 per student per session
- staple remover
- photocopies of the regular polygons - masters on pages 56-63 . All polygons have the same edge length, and all the flaps are the same shape. Use brightly colored, stiff paper, but not card stock. The quantities below will allow each student to build all five regular polyhedra, the dual combination polyhedra, and the truncated polyhedra. If students also build stellated polyhedra, double the number of triangle copies. Few students build all the possible polyhedra, so these quantities may be considered abundant.

polygon	color	copies per student			
		5 regular polyhedra	combination polyhedra	truncated polyhedra	total
triangles	yellow	3	14	3	20
squares	red	1	10	8	19
pentagons	orange	3	8	3	14
hexagons	green	0	0	30	30
octagons	blue	0	0	12	12
decagons	fuchsia	0	0	24	24

- data recorder (page 46) - one copy per student
- standard stapler - to make students' cutting more efficient, staple the photocopies together in packets of three
- wall space - for displaying completed polyhedra
- name cards and markers - Cut five large sheets of poster board into reusable 2½-inch strips to display the official names of the completed polyhedra. Cut construction paper into 2½-inch strips to display the names of the student builders.
- storage space - several shelves in a cabinet to store projects-in-progress
- record sheet - to keep track of which polyhedra each student has built
- instructions - The directions that follow on pages 42 to 55 may be given to the students **verbally**. The directions are written for the instructor and not intended for individual student use.

Many of the words used to describe polyhedra are derived from Greek. You will want to be familiar with the following terms so you can help students understand the names of the various polyhedra. This list includes the prefixes, root words and suffixes used in this unit.

prefixes
- deca - ten
- do - two
- hexa - six
- icosa - twenty
- octa - eight
- penta - five
- poly - many
- tetra - four
- tri - three

suffixes
- hedron - faces

transformations
- rhombi - extra square added
- snub - extra triangle added
- stellation - placing a pyramid on each face
- truncation - cutting off each corner

While this unit can be taught several different ways, it was developed as a unit in which students were given the directions for building the polyhedra verbally. At first they learn how to cut, fold, and staple the 2-dimensional patterns. You will duplicate the patterns (pages 56 to 63) for students, but the instructions on the following pages are just for your information.

It is best to begin with the dodecahedron because it is hard for students to go wrong when learning the basic cutting and stapling skills. The second class should introduce triangles and the third class should introduce squares. Some students like to build cubes, but many think this is too easy. Whenever students finish a polyhedron, you can ask them to begin examining the number of faces, vertices, and edges on these figures. Using the table on page 46, students can record the information and look for patterns.

In successive lessons, students can just try different combinations on their own. As students complete their polyhedra they should show you their constructions so you can record them in your record book and ask them questions. The constructions can then be hung on a bulletin board, which motivates other students to build the same figures or other combinations. Some students like to discover new polyhedra; others like to build polyhedra that are already on display. Every student likes to take home what he or she has built, either at the end of the day or the end of the unit.

Dodecahedron

◆ Students should first build the dodecahedron (12 pentagons), because there is only one way to fit pentagons together, so it is hard to make a mistake.

The Greek name *dodecahedron* indicates the structure of the object. "—hedron" as a suffix refers to "flat surfaces." Using students' knowledge of French or Spanish, ask them what they think the prefix "do-" represents. What number does "deca-" represent? Add these two numbers. How many flat surfaces, or faces, does a dodecahedron have?

◆ Demonstrate the skills of cutting, folding flaps, and stapling three pentagons together. As you cut out three pentagons, remind students that the more carefully they cut, the higher the quality of the finished product. Take special care to cut the corners accurately.

To fold the flaps, hold the pentagon between your thumbs and middle fingers with the dotted lines facing away from you. Use your index fingers to bend a flap down and away from you. Press a strong crease on the line. Repeat with the other four sides. You want the dotted lines to appear on the outside of the finished dodecahedron.

◆ To attach two pentagons, hold together a flap from each one; align the corners, and make the faces flush along the edge. Clamp the flaps between thumb and index finger of one hand, and with the other hand put the silver edge of the stapler on the dotted line midway between the corners. Press firmly, using both hands if necessary. The staple should appear on the line. A little above the line is okay, but if the staple is below the line the fold will not act properly as a hinge; pull such a staple out and try again.

attach

When you add a third pentagon to one of the other two, they all will rest on the tabletop with a gap between them. This prevents regular pentagons from tessellating the plane. That is, you can't fill a surface with regular pentagons without using some other shapes to fill the gaps. When you attach the two closest flaps and close the gap, the magic happens — the three pentagons must lift up off the table surface. Staple those flaps together. You will have one vertex or corner of your dodecahedron.

Continue by adding pentagons in each obvious corner. Remember to connect exactly **three** pentagons at each vertex. The round flaps will make it resemble a round ball, but the dotted lines will clearly show the regular pentagons.

◆ Pass out copies of the pentagons on page 56. Let the students complete their own models. Almost all students third grade or older can finish a dodecahedron in 45 minutes. Student who finish early can count the numbers of vertices and edges on a dodecahedron. Tell students to show you any polyhedra they finish so you can give them credit in your record book.

◆ **Questions for Thought**
- You predicted how many **faces** a dodecahedron has. Were you right?
- How many **vertices**, or corners, does a dodecahedron have?
- How many **edges** does it have?

Tetrahedron, Octahedron and Icosahedron

◆ In the second class, introduce triangles. Cut out 12 triangles for a demonstration. While you are cuttings, tell students that triangles are tricky, because they can combine in three ways – three, four, or five at each vertex. It's easy to get mixed up. For a polyhedron to be **regular**, all its faces must be the same regular polygon and each vertex must look exactly like every other vertex.

◆ Begin your demonstration by stapling three triangles together at two edges, as in the picture. Attach the free edges together. Tell students that this is the top of a **tetrahedron**. To finish just add one more triangle to the bottom.

◆ Staple four triangles together, as pictured below. Again, attach the free edges together. Tell students that this is the top to an **octahedron**. To finish, just add four more triangles to the bottom.

◆ Staple five triangles together, as in the picture below. Again, attach the free edges. Warn students that finishing the **icosahedron** is very difficult because it will be tempting to put four triangles at some vertices and five at others.

◆ Pass out copies of triangles on page 57. Each student will need a packet of three sheets of triangles. Have them work independently to construct all three figures, the tetrahedron, octahedron, and icosahedron.

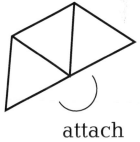

attach

◆ **Tetrahedron** - Students will combine triangles so that three triangles meet at a vertex. They can quickly build a **tetrahedron** – a pyramid with a triangular base. When they count its faces, they will learn the meaning of the Greek prefix *tetra-*.

attach

◆ **Octahedron** - Triangles have small enough angles that four triangles may meet at each vertex. Have students try attaching four triangles together. This is the structure of the **octahedron**. As you build it, make sure that every vertex has four triangles.
Ask students, "How many faces do you expect an octahedron to have? How many edges and vertices?"

attach

◆ **Icosahedron** - It's very easy to make a mistake with this structure. Staple together only groups of five triangles. The Greek word *eikosi-* means "twenty." It may take a longer time to build this structure. When students are done, have them count the edges and vertices.

◆ Walk around and check students' constructions. Whenever you see one that has vertices with four and with five triangles, point out the problem, ask which polyhedron the student intended to build, remove the offending staples, and let the student try again.

◆ As students staple the triangles together point out that if you try to fit six triangles around each vertex, you will find that no magic happens; the triangles stay flat on the table. Since each angle of a regular triangle measures 60°, six of these total 360°, which fill up a circle. Therefore, no regular polyhedron can have six or more triangles at each vertex. This idea is explored further when students study stellation.

◆ Remind students to show you their work whenever they finish a polyhedron so you can give them credit on your record sheet.

◆ Only a few students will complete all three constructions in 45 minutes. Students who don't finish can write their names on the insides of their polyhedra, pile up their cut out shapes, paperclip them together, and store them in a cabinet for the next session.

◆ Students will also enjoy counting the numbers of vertices and edges in these figures.

Question for thought:
Which figure takes more work folding and stapling, the icosahedron or the dodecahedron?

Lesson 3

Cube

◆ During the third class, introduce cubes. Some students like to build cubes, but many think they are too easy. After building the cubes you will examine the patterns in the numbers of faces, edges, and vertices.

◆ Pass out copies of squares on page 58.

◆ Tell students that there is only one more regular polyhedron to build and that is the cube.

 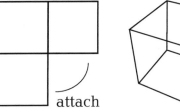

attach

Have students cut out six squares and then use the six squares to build a cube, attaching the patterns so that three faces meet at each vertex. It should not take long for students to construct this figure.

When they are done, their set of regular polyhedra is complete.

◆ Give each student a data recorder (page 46). Write a similar chart on the board. Ask students to agree on the numbers to fill in for faces, edges, and vertices. Then ask the students to find patterns in the numbers. Students really enjoy finding patterns. The correlation of the duals leads naturally to the idea of combining squares and triangles into a cuboctahedron or of combining pentagons and triangles into an icosidodecahedron.

Some of the things that students might discover by examining the patterns in their chart are listed on page 47. You do not have to duplicate this information for students, but you may want to keep probing until they make some of these discoveries.

◆ **Questions for Thought**

How many faces, edges, and vertices does a cube have?

What interesting patterns can you find in these numbers? How do they correlate with each other?

Why are there only five regular polyhedra?

Other lessons

In successive classes, let students try various combinations, some of which work, and some of which don't work. When a student discovers a new pattern that works, tell the whole class the official name of the polyhedron and hang it on the wall display. Write the official name and the name of the student builder below the polyhedron. Hang only well-built polyhedra and try to get one polyhedra from each student. Record the construction in your grade book.

Wait to explain truncation until a student has discovered one of the truncated polyhedra. Then other students are well motivated to discover the other ones. In general, wait to explain each concept (prism, antiprism, pyramid, truncation, stellation, etc.) until a student discovers one of these independently. Some students like to discover new polyhedra, others like to build polyhedra that are already on display.

Data Recorder

Combine the numbers of faces, edges, and vertices that you calculated on earlier projects into the following table.

			faces	edges	vertices
Tetrahedron	3 triangles at each vertex				
Cube	3 squares at each vertex				
Octahedron	4 triangles at each vertex				
Dodecahedron	3 pentagons at each vertex				
Icosahedron	5 triangles at each vertex				

What interesting patterns can you find in these numbers?
How do they correlate to each other?
Can you explain why there are only five regular polyhedra?

      © Prufrock Press Inc. - *Drawing Stars, Building Polyhedra*

Implications

Here are some things students might notice from the table on page 46. We will use these abbreviations:

F = number of faces
E = number of edges   c = number of polygons that touch each vertex.
V = number of vertices   n = number of sides on each face

- All the numbers are even.

- All the edge numbers are multiples of 6.

- $E = Fn/2$
  You divide by 2 because each staple joins two polygon edges into one polyhedron vertex.

- $V = Fn/c$
  You divide by c, because c polygon vertices touch to form one polyhedron vertex.

- $F+V-E = 2$
  This formula was discovered by Leonhard Euler, the greatest mathematician of the eighteenth century. It works for all the polyhedra you will build, and it also works for closed plane networks.

- Both the cube and the octahedron have 12 edges. Therefore, it takes just as much work to build a cube as it does to build an octahedron. There are 24 flaps to cut, fold, and staple, because 6 x 4 = 24 and 8 x 3 = 24.

- Both the dodecahedron and the icosahedron have 30 edges. Therefore, it takes just as much work to build a dodecahedron as it does to build an icosahedron. There are 60 flaps to cut, fold, and staple, because 12 x 5 = 60 and 20 x 3 = 60.

- The cube and the octahedron have switched numbers of faces and vertices – 6 and 8, or 8 and 6. This means that, if you take a cube and draw a dot in the center of each face, and connect these six dots, they will form the vertices of an octahedron that lives inside the cube. Furthermore, if you put dots into the center of each face of this octahedron and connect them, they will form the vertices of a smaller cube. This process may be continued forever toward infinitesimal cubes inside infinitesimal octahedra.

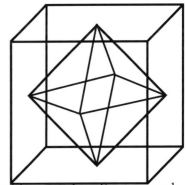

- The dodecahedron and icosahedron also have switched numbers of faces and vertices, so each fits inside the other just like cubes and octahedra.

- Because of the many correlations, the cube and octahedron are called **duals** of each other, and the dodecahedron and icosahedron are also called duals of each other. The tetrahedron is its own dual.

Dual Combination Polyhedra

◆ All of the patterns for polygons have identical edges and flaps, so they can easily be combined. The cube and the octahedron combine into the **cuboctahedron**. In this structure every square is surrounded by triangles, and every triangle is surrounded by squares. The dodecahedron and icosahedron combine into the **icosidodecahedron**. Every pentagon is surrounded by triangles, and every triangle is surrounded by pentagons.

Let students try other combinations. Some combinations work, and some don't work. Real polyhedra have flat surfaces. If the paper has to bend when you build an object, that object doesn't really exist. Almost always, every vertex will look like every other vertex.

◆ For this lesson students will need copies of the triangle, square, and pentagon. Patterns are on pages 56-58.

◆ When students build a new polyhedron, record it in your grade book, tell them the name of the polyhedron and hang it on the wall with their name under it.

◆ The diagrams below show a basic pattern that must be extended to form the entire polyhedron.

Cuboctahedron - Combine squares and triangles so that every square is surrounded by triangles and every triangle is surrounded by squares. Each corner is 4-3-4-3 (square-triangle-square-triangle).

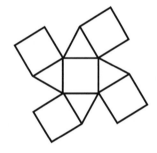

Icosidodecahedron - Combine pentagons and triangles so that every pentagon is surrounded by triangles and every triangle is surrounded by pentagons. Each corner is 5-3-5-3 (pentagon-triangle-pentagon-triangle).

Rhombicuboctahedron - For this structure add extra squares to a cuboctahedron. Six squares are surrounded by squares; twelve other squares are surrounded by alternating squares and triangles. Each corner is 4-4-4-3 (square-square-square-triangle).

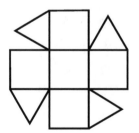

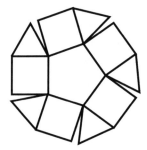

Rhombicosidodecahedron - This structure is constructed by adding extra squares to an icosidodecahedron. Every triangle is surrounded by squares, and every pentagon is surrounded by squares, but every square is surrounded by alternating triangles and pentagons. Each corner is 5-4-3-4 (pentagon-square-triangle-square).

Snub Cube - This figure adds extra triangles to a cuboctahedron. Eight triangles are surrounded by triangles; twenty-four other triangles attach to two triangles and a square. Each corner is 4-3-3-3-3. (square-triangle-triangle-triangle-triangle).
Start with a square.
Staple four triangles around each vertex.
Pick one triangle and staple a triangle to its free flap.
As you go around the other 11 free flaps, alternate attaching a square, then a triangle, then a square.
Continue in this manner.

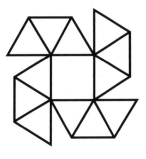

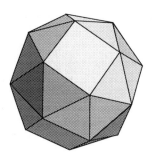

Snub Dodecahedron - Build this polyhedron by adding extra triangles to an icosidodecahedron. Twenty triangles are surrounded by triangles; sixty other triangles attach to two triangles and a pentagon. Each corner is 5-3-3-3-3 (pentagon-triangle-triangle-triangle-triangle).

Truncated Polyhedra

◆ When students are ready, give them this definition:
To **truncate** a polygon is to cut off its corners. When a triangle is truncated, it becomes a hexagon. A truncated square is an octagon. A truncated pentagon is a decagon. One can also truncate any regular and many combination polyhedra by cutting off the vertices. If three polygons meet at a vertex, a triangle appears. If four polygons meet at a vertex, a square appears.

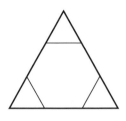

◆ For this lesson, students will need triangles, squares, hexagons, octagons, and decagons, pages 57-61.

◆ For this lesson students will be working independently. You may direct their constructions or let them discover the figures on their own. As they complete a construction, record their work, and give the construction a name and put it on your display board.

◆ Examples
The diagrams below show the basic patterns. Each pattern must be extended to form the whole polyhedron.

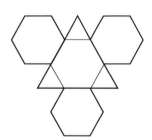

Truncated Tetrahedron - Every triangle is surrounded by hexagons. Around every hexagon are alternating triangles and hexagons. Each corner is 6-6-3 (hexagon-hexagon-triangle).

Truncated Cube - Every triangle is surrounded by three octagons. Around every octagon are alternating triangles and octagons. Each corner is 8-8-3 (octagon-octagon-triangle).

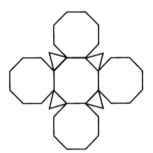
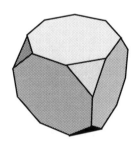

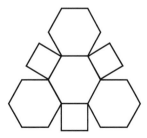

Truncated Octahedron - Every square is surrounded by four hexagons. Around every hexagon are alternating squares and hexagons. Each corner is 6-6-4 (hexagon-hexagon-square).

Truncated Dodecahedron - Every triangle is surrounded by decagons. Around every decagon are alternating triangles and decagons. Each corner is 10-10-3.

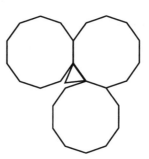 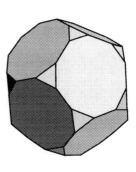

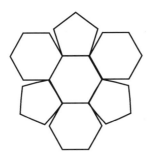

Truncated Icosahedron - In this polyhedron every pentagon is surrounded by hexagons. Around every hexagon are alternating pentagons and hexagons. Each corner is 6-6-5. This polyhedron forms the official soccer ball and also a carbon isotope, C_{60}, known as the "Buckyball," discovered in the 1980's.

Truncated Cuboctahedron - Around each square are alternating hexagons and octagons. Around each hexagon are alternating squares and octagons, and around each octagon are alternating squares and hexagons. Each corner is 8-6-4.

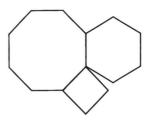

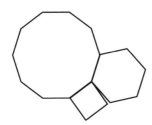

Truncated Icosidodecahedron - Around each square are alternating hexagons and decagons. Around each hexagon are alternating squares and decagons, and around each decagon are alternating squares and hexagons. Each corner is 10-6-4.

Prisms, Antiprisms, and Pyramids

◆ Continue as with previous lessons, letting students work independently. As individuals complete constructions, name the constructions and put them on the display wall.

◆ The following descriptions can be used to guide students' constructions of these three types of polyhedra solids.

Prisms - A prism has a polygon top, an identical polygon base, and parallelograms around the sides. Using squares for the sides, you can construct triangular, square, pentagonal, hexagonal, octagonal, and decagonal prisms.

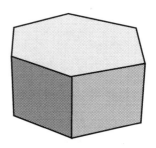

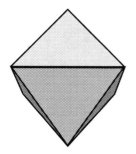 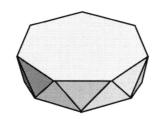

Antiprisms - An antiprism has a polygon top, and identical polygon base, and triangles around the sides. The base is rotated compared to the top, with each corner of the base below the midpoint of a side of the top. Using triangles for the sides, you can construct triangular, square, pentagonal, hexagonal, octagonal, and decagonal antiprisms.

Pyramids - A pyramid has a polygon base surrounded by triangles, all of which have a common upper vertex. Using equilateral triangles, you can construct triangular, square, and pentagonal pyramids.

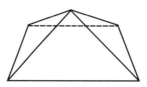 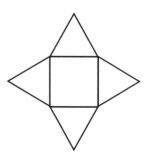

Stellated Polyhedra

Lesson 7

◆ When students are ready, give them this definition for **stellation**:
The word *stellate* comes from the word *stellar*, meaning like a star, and means resembling a star or coming out in points from a center. In a plane, a polygon can be stellated by extending its sides until they meet at points. In essence, specific isosceles triangles are built onto its sides.

◆ In space, a polygon can be stellated by extending its plane faces until their edges meet at points. Effectively, specific regular pyramids are built on each face. Only certain polyhedra can be stellated in this way, and these require pyramids made from isosceles triangles specifically sized for stellation. However, we can approximate formal stellation by building these pyramids out of equilateral triangles. Technically, this process is a form of **cumulation** — combining polyhedra to form compounds.

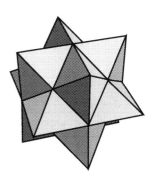

◆ **Stellated Tetrahedron** - Construct four triangular pyramids but leave off their bases. Combine the pyramids so that the empty bases form the faces of a tetrahedron. Curiously, *six* triangles will meet at each inner vertex. This is possible because their edges form ridges and valleys instead of lying flat.

◆ **Stellated Cube** - Construct six square pyramids but leave off their bases. Combine the pyramids so that the empty bases form the faces of a cube.

◆ **Stellated Octahedron** - This structure will require eight triangular pyramids, one for each face. The resulting polyhedron will have *eight* triangles meeting at each inner vertex.

◆ **Stellated Dodecahedro**n - The structure will require 12 pyramids.

◆ **Stellated Icosahedron** - This will require 20 triangular pyramids. It is very hard to build because ten triangles meet at each inner vertex.

◆ **Inverse Stellation** - The pyramids built on each face point *inward* instead of outward.

◆ **Truncated Stellation** - The points of the pyramids on a stellated polyhedra are cut off. Give this idea as a catalyst to your most motivated students and see what they come up with.

◆ **Partial Stellation** - Build pyramids only onto some faces, not others. The partially stellated icosidodecahedron closely resembles the climbing structure in many children's playgrounds.

◆ When students are finished, give their constructions a name and display them with other completed constructions.

Rhombic Polyhedra

Rhombic Dodecahedron

◆ The Construction

The rhombic dodecahedron is the basic form of the garnet crystal. It uses twelve rhombi. Each of these rhombi has diagonals in the ratio $1 : \sqrt{2}$

On the patterns (page 62) the longer diagonals are drawn with dotted lines and the shorter diagonals with solid lines. The dotted diagonals join the acute angles, the solid diagonals join the obtuse angles.

Tell students that three solid diagonals meet at a vertex, but four dotted diagonals meet at a vertex. Never join a dotted diagonal to a solid diagonal.

◆ Questions for Thought:

When the dodecahedron is completed, what figure is formed by the dotted diagonals?
What figure is formed by the solid diagonals?

Answers:

The dotted diagonals form an octahedron, and the solid diagonals form a cube. The rhombic dodecahedron is thus a stellated cube and a stellated octahedron at the same time.

Triacontahedron

◆ The Construction

The triacontahedron uses thirty rhombi. Each of these rhombi has diagonals in the golden ratio, $1 : \dfrac{1+\sqrt{5}}{2}$

On the patterns (page 63) the longer diagonals are drawn with dotted lines and the shorter diagonals with solid lines. The dotted diagonals join the acute angles, the solid diagonals join the obtuse angles.

Tell students that three solid diagonals meet at a vertex, but five dotted diagonals meet at a vertex. Never join a dotted diagonal to a solid diagonal.

◆ Questions for Thought:

When the triacontahedron is completed, what figure is formed by the dotted diagonals?
What figure is formed by the solid diagonals?

Answer:

The dotted diagonals form an icosahedron, and the solid diagonals form a dodecahedron. The rhombic dodecahedron is thus a stellated dodecahedron and a stellated icosahedron at the same time.

Filling Space

◆ Some polyhedra will fit together to fill space. For example, cubes will fit together to fill space, like boxes filling up a storage locker. Space-filling is the three-dimensional analog of tessellation.

◆ The stapling method of attaching polygons allows students to discover combination polyhedra for themselves. However, the flaps get it the way when you try to fit these models together.

◆ To begin the study of space-filling, ask several students to build truncated octahedra using transparent tape instead of staples, cutting off the arc flaps. When completed, these polyhedra can be fitted together to fill space.

The only regular or semi-regular polyhedra that fill space with themselves are:
- cubes
- truncated octahedra
- rhombic dodecahedra.

However, students may enjoy working together to build models to illustrate these combinations that fill space:
- tetrahedra and octahedra
- octahedra and cuboctahedra
- octahedra and truncated cubes
- cubes, truncated octahedra, and truncated cuboctahedra
- cubotahedra, truncated tetrahedra, and truncated octahedra.

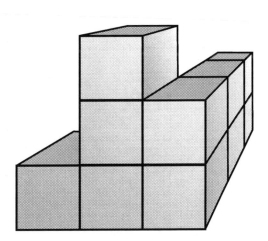

Pentagons

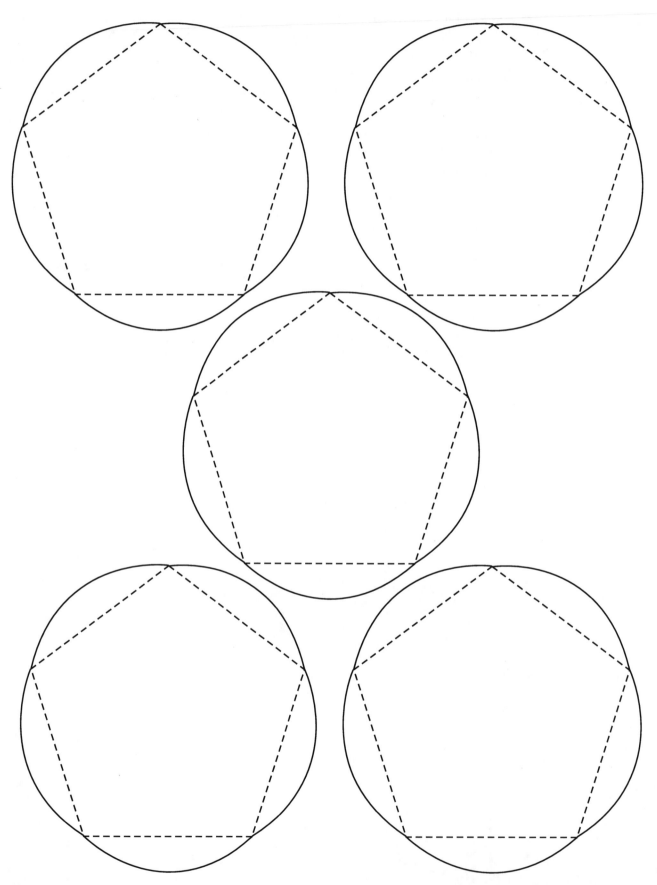

 © Prufrock Press Inc. - *Drawing Stars, Building Polyhedra*

Triangles

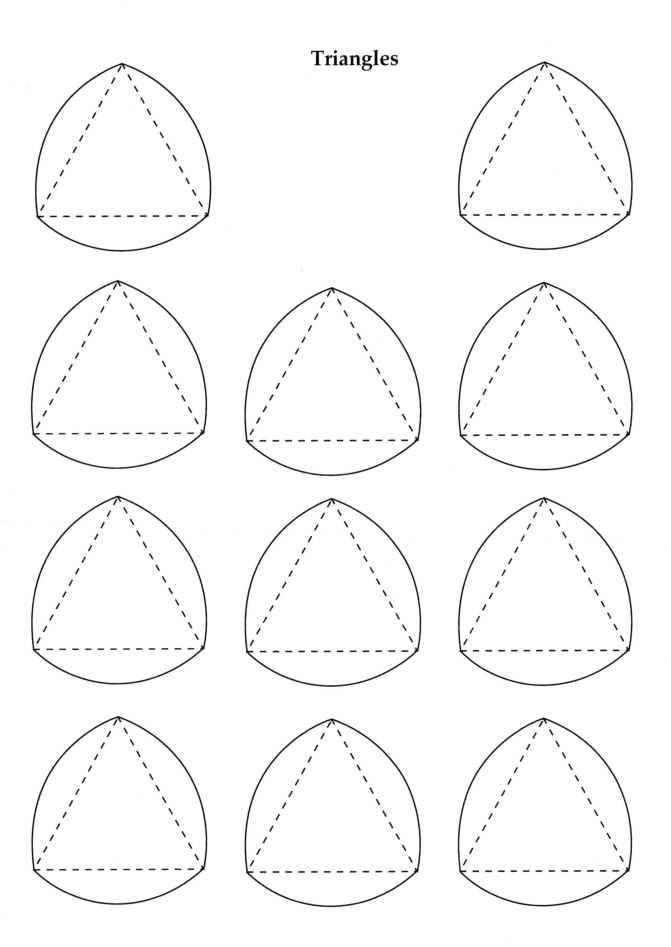

Squares

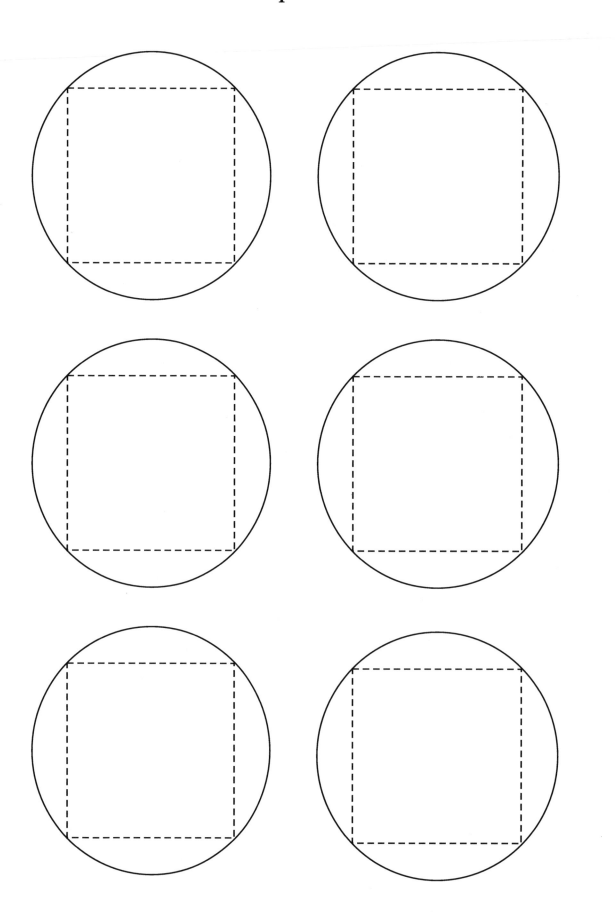

© Prufrock Press Inc. - *Drawing Stars, Building Polyhedra*

Hexagons

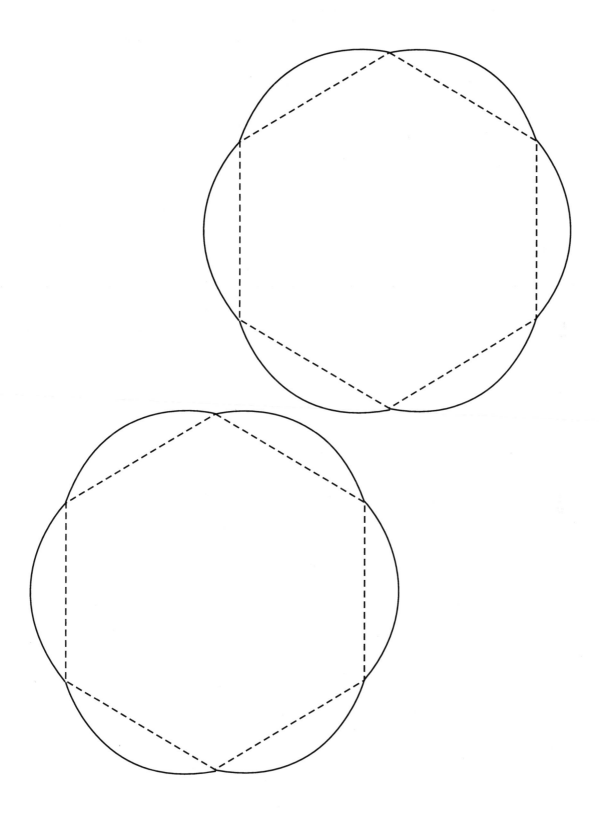

Octagons

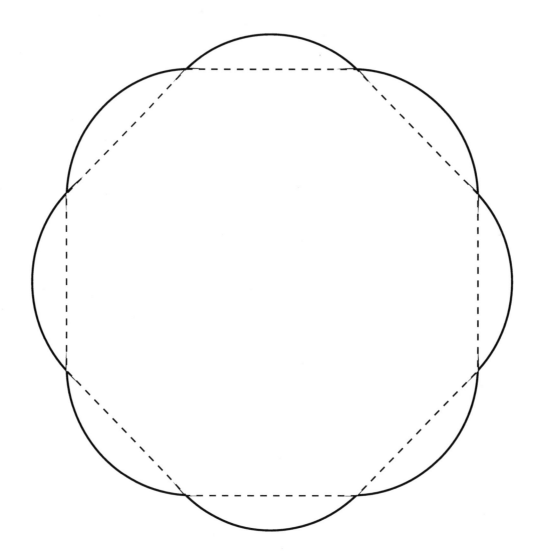

© Prufrock Press Inc. - *Drawing Stars, Building Polyhedra*

Decagons

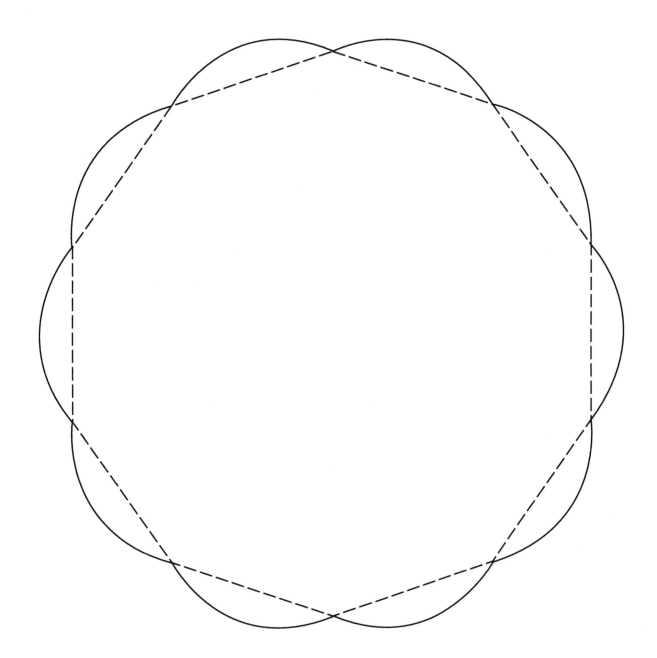

Rhombi
for
Rhombic Dodecahedron
$$D/d = \sqrt{2}$$

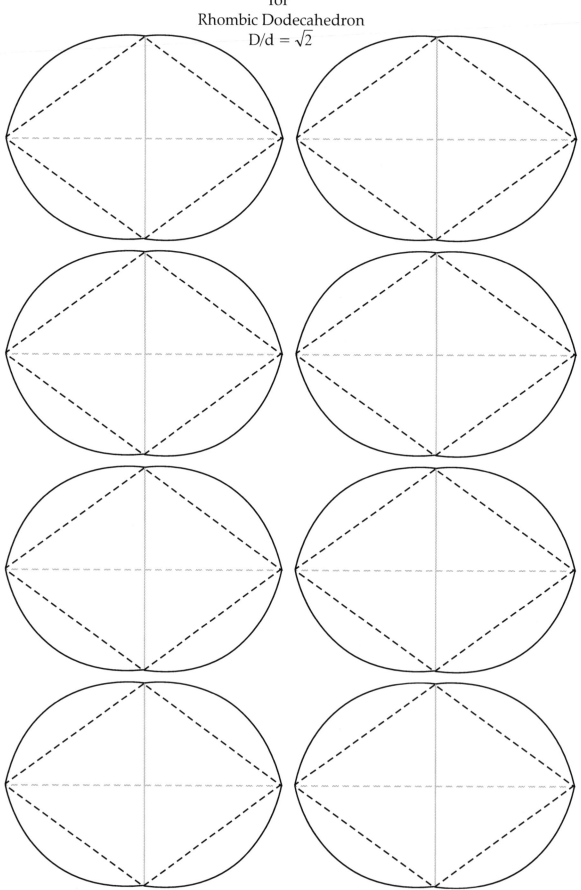

© Prufrock Press Inc. - *Drawing Stars, Building Polyhedra*

Rhombi

for Triacontahedron

D/d = 1.618

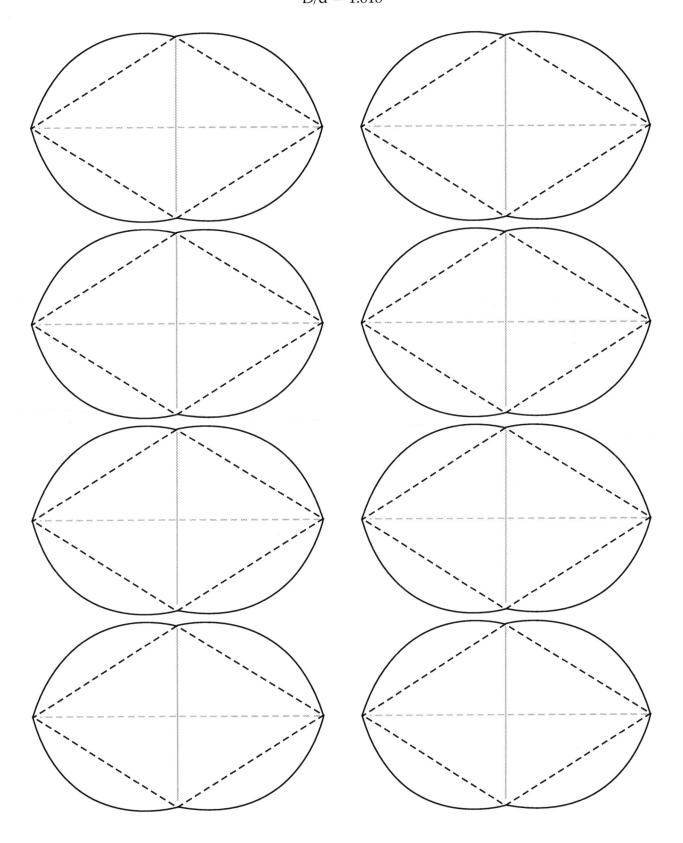

Polyhedra Answers

Lesson 1

"Dos" or "deux" means "two"; "deca" means "ten", as in "decimal" or "decade". Two plus ten is twelve. A dodecahedron has 12 faces, requires 30 staples (has 30 edges), and has 20 vertices.

Lesson 2

The **tetrahedron** has 4 faces, 6 edges, and 4 vertices.
The **octahedron** has 8 faces, 12 edges, and 6 vertices.
The **icosahedron** has 20 faces, 30 edges, and 12 vertices.
The **icosahedron** and the **dodecahedron** have the same number of edges; hence, they require the same amount of folding (60 flaps each) and stapling (30 staples each).
The icosahedron is harder to build only because it is easier to attach the polygons together incorrectly.

Lesson 3

The completed table is as follows:

	faces	edges	vertices
Tetrahedron	4	6	4
Cube	6	12	8
Octahedron	8	12	6
Dodecahedron	12	30	20
Icosahedron	20	30	12

So, why are there only five regular solids? Here is one way to reason. Consider first triangles. We may join at one vertex 3, 4, or 5 triangles. If we try to join six triangles at one vertex, no magic happens. Six triangles exactly fill the gap, because $6 \times 60^\circ = 360^\circ$, a complete circle. And you can't fit more than six triangles, at least if you want your regular polygon to be convex. (Convex means that, if you connect any two vertices, the segment between them will not go outside the polyhedron. If you cram six or more triangles into one vertex, some edges will become ridges and some will become valleys, and the resulting figure cannot be convex.) Similarly, you can fit three squares at one vertex, but if you try four, no magic happens, because $4 \times 90^\circ = 360^\circ$. Again, more squares must produce a non-convex polyhedron. Similarly, you can fit three pentagons at one vertex, but four won't fit. Finally, no magic can happen with hexagons, because if you try to fit three at one vertex they will stay flat, because $3 \times 120^\circ = 360^\circ$. No figures with more sides than hexagons can work, either, because three larger corners will make more than 360°. So, these five are the only regular polyhedra.

Printed in the United States
by Baker & Taylor Publisher Services